Keto Diet Air Fryer Cookbook

Linda Rush

Contents

Chicken Dishes..54

Introduction

Have you missed out on the hype about the ketogenic diet conquering the world recently? All is not lost yet, and this book will help you catch up in no time. In response to increasing popularity of the diet, I created some super-simple and delicious recipes to get you started.

As if that wasn't enough, I am also sharing some practical methods & tricks to make this diet your new lifestyle.

The versatility of the recipes will make it possible for every person to find something suitable for every possible occasion. They are not only meant to be mouth-watering but also to keep you fit and healthy. It is high time you realize that getting rid of large amounts of carbohydrates can do you right.

Strict as it sounds, the ketogenic diet is quite easy to implement, and there is a lot of room for freedom and various adjustments. Options are almost inexhaustible. Its rapidly growing acclaim worldwide only proves that it's arguably the best long-term diet out there at this moment. Don't take my word for it. I challenge you to verify it yourself.

What is a Ketogenic Diet? Start a New Lifestyle

There is a prevalent misconception that carbohydrates are the base fuel our bodies need to function. That is, unfortunately, an unfounded statement, and more and more research is proving it wrong.

Our diet can rely on fats just as well as it can depend on carbohydrates. We benefit from such diet in multiple ways. In the first place, we need to face what may seem to be a drastic change: cutting back on carbohydrates.

Many people think the ketogenic diet is just another 21st-century fitness maniacs' invention. That is, however, far from reality. The roots of this diet are dated back to the early 1920's when the pioneers of this then-unique approach were successfully helping people make their quality of life better.

To get a better understanding of what the ketogenic diet is, let us first analyze what happens in our bodies after consumption of a carbohydrate-rich meal.

To give you an idea, let's, for example, say you just devoured a huge pizza. You are full, happy, and have only provided your body with way more carbohydrates than it needed. Pretty quickly, your body starts the grind of digestion and processing the food, breaking it down into nutrients and separating the rest. The carbs are transformed into glucose, which spikes your insulin level. This is where your energy comes from.

You may now ask what is the problem here? There are many. The whole process raises your blood sugar, you get fatter as the insulin helps your body store fat cells, and your energy level drops drastically not long after eating.

So, how is the ketogenic diet better than regular carbohydrates-based ones? Firstly, as the whole process of breaking down carbohydrates is largely reduced, your blood sugar level low. With a high level of fats accompanied by a moderate amount of proteins, your liver is forced to produce the energy from an alternative source. This process is known as ketosis.

THE KETOSIS

The term Ketosis comes from the so-called Ketones, which are organic compounds, by-products of the process of breaking down the fats in the digestive system.

This fact seeds a lot of doubts amongst more skeptical people, who do not have enough knowledge of the process and consider it detrimental to the body. This is, however, nothing more than a harmful myth preventing them from discovering the scientific facts and the benefits of this diet. Even though your body may experience such a sudden change in the nutrition system as slightly revolutionary, the adaptation process should flow smoothly. Although everybody is different, the shift takes about two weeks in the majority of cases examined.

Benefits and Implementation

In spite of all the controversy around the topic, the ketogenic diet is the best option out there if we want to improve our health without getting rid of some of our favorite, fat-rich dishes.

Loss of Appetite

If you currently cannot imagine living without sugar-stuffed goodies, here comes the good news. Cutting back on sugar will ultimately cause your sugar-cravings to stop. You will be able to control your appetite better, and as a result, it will be easier to stay in good shape. You will quickly realize that the more carbohydrates we eat, the more we feel like they are necessary. The moment you stop the vicious circle, your tastes will inevitably re-adjust, and you will notice that you do not need any carbohydrates or sugar-based food.

Weight Loss

As a result of decreased glucose production, your insulin level will remain low too. This, in turn, will force your liver to remove the extra sodium from the body, helping you to lose weight.

HDL Cholesterol Increase

Another benefit of a fat-based diet is an elevation in the level of so-called good cholesterol – HDL. Cholesterol is mainly associated with the infamous HDL's relative, LDL, which is known for causing various health issues. The HDL, however, many cardiovascular diseases.

Drop in Blood Pressure

If you are suffering from irregular or elevated blood pressure, which in the long run may cause serious health issues such as stroke and heart disease, the ketogenic diet might be a perfect solution for you.

Lower Risk of Diabetes

As explained before, a low glucose level will also keep your insulin level at a low level. The ketogenic diet is your ally in the prevention of diabetes, which is one of the deadliest diseases of our time.

Improved Brain Function

More and more studies have been carried out proving that our mind performs better having ketones as fuel. It is also noteworthy that over time, as we age, our brain is not able to efficiently use glucose as an energy source as it did before.

Longevity

Although more long-term research has yet to be conducted, starting the ketogenic diet may significantly expand your lifespan. This is since the oxidative stress level is significantly decreased, which directly affects our life expectancy.

Limitations on the Keto Plate

The most significant advantage of being on a keto diet is that you are neither strictly limited to what you can eat, nor when you should eat. Starving yourself will not come into play either. In fact, unlike the majority of other diets, this one is not about limiting the quantity but instead changing the quality.

The only rule to follow is straightforward. Reducing carbohydrates, increasing fats, keeping protein intake at a moderate level. That does not mean you have to go to extremes and measure every single bite you take. Sticking to the rule of 75% fats /20 % proteins /5 % carbohydrates is a good starting point.

Another simple rule you can follow if you like everything measured is this one: consume no more than 20 grams of carbohydrates per day.

It's entirely up to you how you divide this daily portion. If you have a carbo-whim at a given moment, fair enough. Eat it all at once. Just remember the rule of having other meals during the day.

The recipes in the book are diversified, ranging from zero to a few grams of carbohydrates.

Foods to Eat when on a Ketogenic Diet

There are certain foods that will enrich your diet, providing you with a high content of fat, serving as a long-lasting energy source.

- Whole Eggs
- All kinds of meat
- Fish and Seafood
- Bacon
- Sausage
- Avocados
- Leafy Greens
- Seeds
- Non-Starchy Vegetables: Cucumber, Zucchini, Asparagus, Broccoli, Onion, Brussel Sprouts, Cabbage, Tomatoes, Eggplant, Sea Weed, Peppers, Squash
- Full-Fat Dairy (heavy cream, yogurt, sour cream, cheese, etc.)
- Nuts. They are full of healthy fats, especially macadamia nuts, pecans, and almonds. These should be ones to choose first. On the flipside, though, pay attention to pistachios, chestnuts, and cashews, as they are carbs-rich compared to rest of the nuts.

Foods to Avoid

Despite having quite a lot of freedom on this diet, there will be a few things that must be replaced or removed if you want to approach this change seriously. Most of them are devoid of nutritional value and cause lots of adverse effects on your body.

- Sugar
- Diet Soda
- Starchy Vegetables. Potatoes, beans, parsnips, legumes, peas, and corn. They, unfortunately, contain lots of carbs. They must be removed. Adding some starch, however, if your daily carb limit allows, is permitted.
- Grains. Rice, wheat, and everything made from grains, such as pasta or bread, must be avoided.
- Trans Fats
- Refined Oils and Fats (corn oil, canola oil, etc.)

Keto Swap Foods

To make your start easier, you may consider using certain 'tricks.' It means that each 'forbidden' item on the list has a healthier equivalent you may swap it for. We call it 'keto swaps.' If you master them, your cooking will become more comfortable and faster. With such help, you will not have to dwell upon what to cook to make it keto-adapted.

Bread and Buns - Bread made from nut flour, mushroom caps, cucumber slices

Wraps and tortillas - Wraps and tortillas made from nut flour, lettuce leaves, kale leaves

Pasta and spaghetti - Spiralized veggies such as zoodles, spaghetti squash, etc.

Lasagna Noodles - Zucchini or eggplant slices

Rice - Cauliflower rice (ground in a food processor)

Mashed potatoes - Mashed cauliflower or other veggies

Hash browns - Cauliflower or spaghetti squash

Flour - Coconut flour, nut flour

Breadcrumbs - Almond flour or Pork rinds

Pizza crust - Crust made with allowed flour, cauliflower crust

French fries - Carrot sticks, turnip fries, zucchini fries

Potato chips - Zucchini chips, kale chips

Croutons - Bacon bits, nuts, sunflower seeds, flax crackers

What is the Air Fryer?

A short history of the Air Fryer

Air Frying is a unique method of cooking in a very well-sealed pot that helps to fry healthy food. The heat that is built up inside the Air Fryer allows any ingredients to reach a higher temperature before actually being fried. It also uses a tiny quantity of oil.

The French physicist, Denis Papin, invented this method in 1679. It was only put into practice and used in cooking during World War II. The main reason that people used the Air Fryer was to save as much fuel as possible and also to fry food in a shorter time.

The structure and use of the Air Fryer

Generally, any Air Fryer is made of the following parts:

A fry Basket, a basket Release Button, a basket Handle, an outer Basket, an outer and Fry Basket Assembly,

A food Separator, an air Intake vent, a digital Control, an air Outlet Vent, the main Unit Housing

Benefits of Air Fryer

The principle of the Air Fryer is relatively simple. The heating point inside the Air Fryer depends on the atmospheric pressure. One of the specific qualities of the Air Fryer is that this cooking method helps obtain light recipes with no fat that can still be very tasty. For instance, components like corn, peas, cauliflower, and broccoli can be cooked and fried in a short time.

What to cook in the Air Fryer?

Air Fryer allows us to cook almost everything, an infinite number of dishes. We can use the Air Fryer to cook meat, vegetables, poultry, fruit, fish and a wide variety of desserts. It is possible to prepare entire meals, from appetizers to main courses to desserts. Furthermore, the Air Fryer cooks even delicious sweets and cakes.

Air Fryer Principle – Caution use

It will help if you read all the instructions before using the Air Fryer. Remember not to place the appliance against the wall or any another appliance.

You should leave around 5 inches of space free on each side of the machine.

Remember not to place any object on top of the appliance.

Try not to use the appliance for any other reason or purpose than the ones described in the manual.

Try not to use any accessible surfaces that will become hot during the use.

Most importantly, do not place the appliance near any combustible things or materials.

Cooking tips

Any food that is quickly cooked in convection, a microwave, or even a toaster oven may also be prepared in an Air Fryer.

Tiny ingredients require a shorter frying time in comparison with larger ingredients.

If you want to have a crispy surface, you can use olive oil or a non-stick oil. Never add too much oil to the heating chamber. Never overfill it, because it will damage the Air Fryer.

Breakfast

<u>Creamy Egg Avocado Salad</u>

Servings: 3

Prep + Cook Time: 7 minutes

NUTRITIONAL INFO PER SERVING:

Calories 472; Carbs 17.3g; Net Carbs 4.2g; Fiber 13.2g; Protein 17g; Fat 41g

INGREDIENTS:

6 COOKED EGGS

2 PEELED AND CHOPPED AVOCADOS

2 CUPS CHOPPED TOMATOES

½ CUP CUT RED ONION

SALT AND PEPPER, TO TASTE

2 TBSP KETO MAYO

2 TBSP SOUR CREAM

1 TBSP LEMON JUICE

6 DROPS HOT SAUCE

DIRECTIONS:

1. In the basket of the Air Fryer, place thinly sliced eggs.

2. Add the tomatoes, the red onion, salt, and pepper.

3. Set the timer to 7 minutes and the heat to 340° F.

4. When ready, transfer the ingredients into a bowl.

5. Stir in the mayo, the sour cream, the lemon juice, and the hot sauce.

6. Garnish with avocado.

Asparagus Omelet

Servings: 2

Prep + Cook Time: 8 minutes

NUTRITIONAL INFO PER SERVING:

Calories 287; Carbs 3g; Net Carbs 2g; Fiber 0.2g; Protein 15g; Fat 23g

INGREDIENTS:

3 EGGS

1 TBSP PARMESAN CHEESE

2 TBSP WARM WATER

A PINCH OF SALT

A PINCH OF BLACK PEPPER

2 TBSP NON-STICK SPRAY

5 STEAMED ASPARAGUS TIPS

DIRECTIONS:

1. Start by whisking the eggs, the cheese, the water, salt, and pepper in a large bowl, then blend them.
2. Spray a pan with a non-stick spray and steam.
3. Then add to the Air Fryer basket.
4. Pour the egg mixture into the basket and add the asparagus.
5. Set the temperature to 320° F and cook for 5 minutes.

Air Cooked Eggs

Servings: 3

Prep + Cook Time: 8 minutes

NUTRITIONAL INFO PER SERVING:

Calories 223; Carbs 6.7g; Net Carbs 3.1g; Fiber 3.2g; Protein 18g; Fat 13g

INGREDIENTS:

1 LB SPINACH

4 OZ SLICED HAM

4 EGGS

1 TBSP OLIVE OIL

4 TBSP WATER

SALT AND BLACK PEPPER, TO TASTE

DIRECTIONS:

1. Preheat the Air Fryer to 360° F, if needed. Butter 4 ramekins.

2. In each ramekin, place the spinach, one egg, an ounce of ham, a tablespoon of water, salt, and pepper.

3. Line the ramekins in the Air Fryer's basket.

4. Set the timer to 10 minutes (6-7 minutes for runny eggs).

Scrambled Eggs

Serving: 1

Prep + Cook Time: 6 minutes

NUTRITIONAL INFO PER SERVING:

Calories 180; Carbs 0.6g; Net Carbs 0.2g; Fiber 0g; Protein 11g; Fat 14g

INGREDIENTS:

2 EGGS

¼ OZ MELTED BUTTER

SALT AND PEPPER

DIRECTIONS:

5. Break and whisk the eggs. Preheat the Air Fryer to 240° F.

6. Add butter to Air Fryer's basket, and place the eggs. Cook for 6 minutes.

7. Serve the eggs with cheese and tomatoes (optional).

Eastern Beet and Feta Salad

Servings: 4

Prep + Cook Time: 45 minutes

NUTRITIONAL INFO PER SERVING:

Calories 225; Carbs 11.3g; Net Carbs 6.2g; Fiber 4.2g; Protein 7g; Fat 16g

INGREDIENTS:

4 LARGE BEETS, STEMS TRIMMED

2 TBSP OLIVE OIL

SALT AND PEPPER, TO TASTE

3 TBSP RED WINE VINEGAR

¼ CUP MINCED RED ONION

2 CLOVES MINCED GARLIC

1 ½ TBSP DIJON MUSTARD

½ TBSP LIQUID STEVIA

1 TBSP MINCED FRESH PARSLEY

1 TBSP MINCED FRESH MARJORAM

½ TBSP MINCED THYME LEAVES

2 CUPS MIXED BABY LETTUCES

3/4 CUP CRUMBLED FETA CHEESE

DIRECTIONS:

1. Preheat the Air Fryer to 390°F.
2. Wash the beets thoroughly and dry them.
1. Place the beets on aluminum foil and add to a baking sheet.
2. Drizzle with oil, and cook for 20 minutes.
3. Season with salt and pepper.
4. Close up with aluminum foil the beets.
5. Cook in an oven until tender.

6. Then transfer to the Air Fryer and cook the beets for 45 minutes.

7. Remove them and place in the fridge.

8. Meanwhile in a bowl, mix the onion, the garlic, the mustard, and the stevia.

9. Whisk the ingredients until they are thoroughly combined.

10. Stir in the herbs and season with salt and pepper.

11. When the beets are chilled, cut them into slices of half an inch.

12. Garnish with baby lettuce.

Pumpkin Pie French Toast

Servings: 4

Prep + Cook Time: 26 minutes

NUTRITIONAL INFO PER SERVING:

Calories 267; Carbs 7.3g; Net Carbs 3.2g; Fiber 0.2g; Protein 8g; Fat 19g

INGREDiENTS:

2 LARGE, BEATEN EGGS

¼ CUP WATER

¼ CUP PUMPKIN PURÉE

¼ TSP PUMPKIN PIE SPICES

4 SLICES LOW-CARB BREAD

¼ CUP BUTTER

DIRECTIONS:

1. In a large bowl, mix the eggs, the water, the pumpkin, and the pie spice.

2. Whisk until you obtain a smooth mixture.

3. Dip both sides of the bread in the egg mixture.

4. Place the rack inside the Air Fryer's cooking basket.

5. Set the temperature to 340° F and set time to 10 minutes.

6. Serve the pumpkin pie with butter.

Roasted Cabbage Salad

Servings: 3

Prep + Cook Time: 30 minutes

NUTRITIONAL INFO PER SERVING:

Calories 145; Carbs 10.3g; Net Carbs 5.2g; Fiber 3.2g; Protein 3g; Fat 10g

INGREDIENTS:

2 TBSP OLIVE OIL

½ HEAD GREEN CABBAGE CUT INTO 4 WEDGES

A PINCH OF GARLIC POWDER

A PINCH OF RED PEPPER FLAKES

A PINCH OF GROUND BLACK PEPPER

2 SMALL HALVED LEMONS

DIRECTIONS:

1. Preheat the Air Fryer to 390°F.
2. Brush the sides of each of the cabbage wedges with the olive oil.
3. Sprinkle with garlic powder and add a pinch of red pepper flakes and salt.
4. Roast the cabbage wedges in the Air Fryer for 30 minutes.
7. Make sure to flip them at least once.
5. Squeeze lemon juice and enjoy its delicious taste!
6. Put the soup back in the fryer and stir continually for 2 minutes.
7. Top with cream and parsley.
8. Put soup back to the Air Fryer and heat it for 1 minute.
9. Sprinkle with white and black pepper if you like.

Pumpkin Seed Brown Bread

Servings: 4

Prep + Cook Time: 28 minutes

NUTRITIONAL INFO PER SERVING:

Calories 396; Carbs 9.3g; Net Carbs 2.8g; Fiber 8.2g; Protein 13g; Fat 36g

INGREDIENTS:

8 OZ ALMOND FLOUR

1 OZ LIQUID STEVIA

3 OZ WATER

1 EGG

2 TBSP BUTTER

DIRECTIONS:

1. Combine flour, stevia, and water.
2. Keep mixing the components with hands.
3. Add the butter and knead the mixture very well.
4. Let bread dough rest, keep warm and covered, for about 2 hours until it grows in size.
5. Then, divide the dough into small balls of 1 oz. each and place in baking paper.
6. Brush the balls with the egg.
7. Let the dough rest again for 30-40 minutes.
8. Place dough balls in a tray.
9. Cook in the Air Fryer at 330° F, until brown and crispy.

Roasted Asparagus Salad

Servings: 3

Prep + Cook Time: 10 minutes

NUTRITIONAL INFO PER SERVING:

Calories 232; Carbs 13.3g; Net Carbs 6.2g; Fiber 6.2g; Protein 10g; Fat 16g

INGREDIENTS:

1 LB TRIMMED AND CUT ASPARAGUS

2 YELLOW PEPPERS, CUT AND CUBED

¼ CUP TOASTED ALMONDS

½ CUP GRATED PARMESAN CHEESE

2 TBSP OLIVE OIL

2 TBSP DIJON MUSTARD

2 CLOVES GARLIC

2 TBSP LIME JUICE

1 TBSP HOT SAUCE

DIRECTIONS:

1. Preheat the Air Fryer to 390° F.
2. Mix the asparagus and the bell peppers with 1 tbsp. of olive oil.
3. Cook them for 10 minutes in the Air Fryer
4. Remove from the heat and add the almonds and the parmesan cheese.
5. In another bowl, mix 1 tbsp. of olive oil, the mustard, the garlic, the lime juice, and the hot sauce.
6. Combine the 2 groups of food and serve.

Roasted Radish and Mozzarella Salad

Servings: 4

Prep + Cook Time: 35 minutes

NUTRITIONAL INFO PER SERVING:

Calories 235; Carbs 6.3g; Net Carbs 2.6g; Fiber 3.2g; Protein 19g; Fat 15g

INGREDIENTS:

1 LB RADISHES WITH THEIR TOPS

2 TBSP OLIVE OIL

1 TSP SALT

½ TSP GROUND BLACK PEPPER

½ LB MOZZARELLA

2 TBSP BALSAMIC OIL

DIRECTIONS:

1. Wash the radishes under cold running water.

2. Rinse and pat dry the radishes using a paper towel.

3. Make sure to rim the wilted stems from the radish.

4. In a large bowl, place the radishes and drizzle with oil, a pinch of salt and a pinch of pepper.

5. Transfer the ingredients to the Air Fryer.

6. Set the heat to 350° F and the timer to 35 minutes.

7. Once cooked, top with the cheese.

Thai Omelet

Servings: 3

Prep + Cook Time: 20 minutes

NUTRITIONAL INFO PER SERVING:

Calories 253; Carbs 5.3g; Net Carbs 2.2g; Fiber 1.2g; Protein 11g; Fat 11g

INGREDIENTS:

4 EGGS

2 TBSP FISH SAUCE

2 TBSP WHITE PEPPER POWDER

JUICE FROM ½ LIME

2 CLOVES GARLIC

1 MINCED SHALLOT

½ CUP FINELY CUT SAUSAGE

1 HANDFUL FRESH SPINACH

1 FRESH GREEN ONION

CILANTRO, TO GARNISH

DIRECTIONS:

7. Heat oil in a pan. Crack the eggs into a large bowl.

8. Add the fish sauce and the pepper.

9. Whisk until bubbles start to appear in the mixture.

10. Add the remaining ingredients and keep whisking until well combined.

11. Pour the obtained mixture inside the pan and place it in the basket of the Air Fryer.

12. Cook for 10 minutes at 340°F. Sprinkle with cilantro.

Side Dishes and Snacks

Onion Rings

Servings: 3

Prep + Cook Time: 10 minutes

NUTRITIONAL INFO PER SERVING:

Calories 165; Carbs 6.3g; Net Carbs 4.7g; Fiber 012g; Protein 6g; Fat 8g

INGREDIENTS:

1 ONION

1 ½ CUPS ALMOND FLOUR

1 TBSP BAKING POWDER

1 EGG

1 CUP COCONUT MILK

¾ CUP PORK RINDS

DIRECTIONS:

1. Preheat the Air Fryer for 10 minutes, if needed.
2. Cut the onion into slices and then separate them into rings.
3. In a bowl, add the flour, the baking powder, and the salt.
4. Whisk the eggs and the milk and combine with the flour.
5. Dip the floured onion rings into the batter to coat it.
6. Spread the pork rinds on a plate and dredge all the rings in the rinds.
7. Cook the rings in the Air Fryer for around 10 minutes at 360° F.

Roasted Vegetables with Garlic

Servings: 4

Prep + Cook Time: 12 minutes

NUTRITIONAL INFO PER SERVING:

Calories 212; Carbs 15.3g; Net Carbs 7.8g; Fiber 5.2g; Protein 10g; Fat 13g

INGREDIENTS:

1 LB TOMATOES

1 LB GREEN PEPPER

1 MEDIUM ONION

3 CLOVES GARLIC

½ TBSP SALT

1 TBSP CORIANDER POWDER

1 TBSP LEMON JUICE

1 TBSP OLIVE OIL

2 OZ BLACK OLIVE

3 COOKED EGGS

DIRECTIONS:

1. Line the pepper, the tomatoes and the onion in the basket.
2. Cook for 5 minutes, then flip around and cook for 5 more minutes, at 300°F.
3. Remove them from the Air Fryer and peel their skin.
4. Place the vegetables in a blender and sprinkle with the salt and the coriander powder.
5. Blend to a smooth mixture.
6. Top with the cooked eggs and sprinkle olive oil.

Crispy Eggplant Fries

Servings: 3

Prep + Cook Time: 20 minutes

NUTRITIONAL INFO PER SERVING:

Calories 265; Carbs 17.3g; Net Carbs 4,2g; Fiber 13.2g; Protein 4g; Fat 21g

INGREDIENTS:

2 EGGPLANTS

¼ CUP ALMOND FLOUR

¼ CUP OLIVE OIL

½ CUP WATER

DIRECTIONS:

1. Preheat the Air Fryer to 390°F, if needed.
2. Cut the eggplants in slices of half inch each.
3. In a big bowl, mix the flour, olive oil, water, and the eggplants.
4. Slowly coat the eggplants.
5. Cook for around 12 minutes or until they start to brown.
6. Repeat this process until all eggplant slices are cooked.
7. Serve with yogurt or tomato sauce.

Crispy Kale Chips

Servings: 2

Prep + Cook Time: 10 minutes

NUTRITIONAL INFO PER SERVING:

Calories 167; Carbs 5.3g; Net Carbs 2.9g; Fiber 2.1g; Protein 5g; Fat 15g

INGREDIENTS:

2 TBSP OLIVE OIL

4 CUPS STEMMED AND PACKED KALE

1 TSP VEGAN SEASONING

1 TBSP YEAST FLAKES

SEA SALT, TO TASTE

DIRECTIONS:

1. In a bowl, mix the oil, the kale and the vegan seasoning.
2. Add the yeast and mix well. Dump the coated kale in the Air Fryer's basket.
3. Set the heat to 370° F and time to 5 minutes.
4. Shake after 3 minutes. Serve sprinkled with sea salt.

Crispy Crumbed Chicken Tenderloins

Servings: 4

Prep + Cook Time: 15 minutes

NUTRITIONAL INFO PER SERVING:

Calories 312; Carbs 0.8g; Net Carbs 0.8g; Fiber 0.2g; Protein 21g; Fat 17g

INGREDIENTS:

2 TBSP OIL

2 OZ PORK RINDS

1 LARGE WHISKED EGG

6 CHICKEN TENDERLOINS

DIRECTIONS:

1. Preheat the air fryer to 365° F. Combine the oil with the pork rinds.

2. Keep mixing and stirring until the mixture gets crumbly.

3. Dip the chicken in the egg wash. Dip the chicken in the rinds mix, making sure it is evenly and fully covered. Cook for 12 minutes. Serve the dish and enjoy its crispy taste!

Garlic Tomatoes

Servings: 2

Prep + Cook Time: 20 minutes

NUTRITIONAL INFO PER SERVING:

Calories 135; Carbs 9.3g; Net Carbs 6.7g; Fiber 2.2g; Protein 1g; Fat 5g

INGREDIENTS:

4 TOMATOES

1 TBSP OLIVE OIL

SALT AND BLACK PEPPER, TO TASTE

1 MINCED CLOVE GARLIC

½ TBSP DRIED THYME

3 TBSP VINEGAR

DIRECTIONS:

1. Preheat the Air Fryer to 390° F, if needed.

2. Cut the tomatoes in half, and remove the seeds.

3. Put them in a big bowl and toss well with the oil, the salt, the pepper, the garlic, and the thyme.

4. Place them in the Air Fryer and cook them for 15 minutes.

5. Drizzle with vinegar and serve.

Zucchini Fries

Servings: 3

Prep + Cook Time: 15 minutes

NUTRITIONAL INFO PER SERVING:

Calories 193; Carbs 0.6g; Net Carbs 0.3g; Fiber 0.2g; Protein 1g; Fat 21g

INGREDIENTS:

4 LARGE ZUCCHINI

¼ CUP ALMOND FLOUR

¼ CUP OLIVE OIL

¼ CUP WATER

A PINCH OF SALT

DIRECTIONS:

1. Preheat the Air Fryer to 390°F. Cut the zucchini to a half inch by 3 inches.
2. In a large bowl, mix the flour, the olive oil, the water, and the zucchini.
3. Mix very well and coat the zucchini. Line the zucchini fries in the Air Fryer and cook for 15 minutes. Recommended to serving with full-fat greek yogurt and garlic paste.

Delicious Fried Calamari

Servings: 4

Prep + Cook Time: 10 minutes |

NUTRITIONAL INFO PER SERVING:

Calories 233; Carbs 0.7g; Net Carbs 0.7g; Fiber 0.2g; Protein 32g; Fat 11g

INGREDIENTS:

1 LB CALAMARI (SQUID), CUT IN RINGS

¼ CUP ALMOND FLOUR

2 LARGE BEATEN EGGS

1 CUP PORK RINDS

DIRECTIONS:

1. Coat the calamari rings with the flour. Dip the calamari in the mixture of the eggs. Then, dip in the pork rinds. Cool in the fridge for 2 hours.

2. Line them in the Air Fryer and apply oil generously. Cook for 10 minutes on 380° F. Serve with garlic mayo or lemon wedges.

Salmon Balls

Servings: 2

Prep + Cook Time: 15 minutes

NUTRITIONAL INFO PER SERVING:

Calories 389; Carbs 3.3g; Net Carbs 1.6g; Fiber 1.7g; Protein 25g; Fat 32g

INGREDIENTS:

6 OZ TINNED SALMON

1 LARGE EGG

4 TBSP CHOPPED CELERY

4 TBSP SPRING ONION, SLICED

1 TBSP DILL, FRESH AND CHOPPED

½ TBSP GARLIC POWDER

5 TBSP PORK RINDS

3 TBSP OLIVE OIL

DIRECTIONS:

1. Preheat the Air Fryer to 370°F.

2. In a large bowl, mix salmon, egg, celery, onion, dill, and garlic powder.

3. Shape the mixture into golf ball size balls and roll them in pork rinds.

4. Heat the oil in a skillet. Add the salmon balls and slowly flatten them.

5. Then transfer them to the air fryer and fry for about 10 minutes.

Crispy Almond Flour Cheesy Lings

Servings: 4

Prep + Cook Time: 5 minutes

NUTRITIONAL INFO PER SERVING:

Calories 173; Carbs 5.7g; Net Carbs 2.5g; Fiber 3.2g; Protein 6g; Fat 14g

INGREDIENTS:

1 CUP ALMOND FLOUR

1 TSP BAKING POWDER

¼ TSP CHILI POWDER

1 TSP BUTTER

3 TBSP GRATED CHEDDAR CHEESE

HOT SAUCE, TO SERVE

DIRECTIONS:

1. Mix the flour and the baking powder.
2. Add salt, chili powder, butter, grated cheese, and a few drops of water to the mixture.
3. Make sure to make a stiff dough.
4. Knead the dough for a while.
5. Now, sprinkle a small quantity of flour on the table.
6. Take a rolling pin and roll the dough.
7. Then, cut into any shape wanted.
8. Preheat the air fryer to 370° F. Set the time to 4 minutes and line the cheese lings in the basket.
9. Serve with hot sauce!

Asparagus Cheesy Fries

Servings: 4

Prep + Cook Time: 32 minutes /

NUTRITIONAL INFO PER SERVING:

Calories 213; Carbs 7.3g; Net Carbs 4.1g; Fiber 2.9g; Protein 19g; Fat 12g

INGREDIENTS:

1 LB. ASPARAGUS SPEARS

¼ CUP ALMOND FLOUR

1 CUP PORK RINDS

½ CUP PARMESAN CHEESE, GRATED

2 EGGS, BEATEN

SALT AND PEPPER, TO TASTE

DIRECTIONS:

1. Preheat the air fryer to 380 degrees, if needed.
2. Combine the pork rinds and the Parmesan cheese in a small bowl.
3. Season with salt and pepper.
4. Line a baking sheet with parchment paper.
5. First, dip half of the asparagus spears into the flour, then into the eggs, and finally coat with pork rinds.
6. Arrange them on the sheet and cook for about 9 to 10 minutes.
7. Repeat with the remaining spears.

Cheesy Croquettes with Prosciutto

Servings: 6

Prep + Cook Time: 45 minutes /

NUTRITIONAL INFO PER SERVING:

Calories 346; Carbs 8.3g; Net Carbs 5.2g; Fiber 0g; Protein 23g; Fat 25g

INGREDIENTS:

1 LB. CHEDDAR CHEESE

12 SLICES PROSCIUTTO

1 CUP ALMOND FLOUR

2 EGGS, BEATEN

4 TBSP OLIVE OIL

1 CUP PORK RINDS

DIRECTIONS:

1. Cut the cheese into 6 equal pieces.
2. Wrap each piece of cheese with 2 prosciutto slices.
3. Place them in the freezer just enough to set. I left mine for about 5 minutes.
4. Note that they mustn't be frozen.
5. Meanwhile, preheat your air fryer to 380 degrees F.
6. Dip the croquettes into the flour first then the egg, and then coat them with the pork rinds.
7. Place the olive oil in the basket of the air fryer and cook the croquettes for 7 minutes, or until golden.

Cheesy Mozzarella Stick

Servings: 3

Prep + Cook Time: 40-45 minutes /

NUTRITIONAL INFO PER SERVING:

Calories 314; Carbs 3.3g; Net Carbs 1.5g; Fiber 1.7g; Protein 36g; Fat 16g

INGREDIENTS:

8 OZ MOZZARELLA CHEESE

1 TSP GARLIC POWDER

1 EGG

1 CUP PORK RINDS

½ TSP SALT

2 TBSP OLIVE OIL

DIRECTIONS:

1. Cut the mozzarella into 6 strips.
2. Whisk the egg along with the salt and garlic powder.
3. Dip the mozzarella into the egg mixture first, and then into the pork rinds.
4. Arrange them on a platter and place in the freezer for about 30 min.
5. Preheat the air fryer to 360 degrees.
6. Drizzle olive oil into the Air Fryer.
7. Arrange the mozzarella sticks in the air fryer and cook for 5 minutes.
8. Flip at least twice, to ensure that they will cook evenly on all sides.

Appetizers

Cooked Tomato Nest

Servings: 2

Prep + Cook Time: 20 minutes |

NUTRITIONAL INFO PER SERVING:

Calories 302; Carbs 8.3g; Net Carbs 4.2g; Fiber 3.2g; Protein 30g; Fat 16g

INGREDIENTS:

2 TOMATOES

4 EGGS

1 CUP MOZZARELLA CHEESE

A FEW BASIL LEAVES

1 TBSP OLIVE OIL

SALT AND BLACK PEPPER, TO TASTE

DIRECTIONS:

1. Preheat the Air Fryer to 360° F.
2. Cut each tomato into two halves and place them in a bowl.
3. Season with salt and pepper.
4. Place cheese around the bottom of the tomatoes and add basil leaves.
5. Break one egg in each tomato slice.
6. Top with cheese and drizzle with olive oil.
7. Set the temperature to 360° F and cook the tomatoes for 20 minutes.

Chopped Liver with Eggs

Servings: 4

Prep + Cook Time: 15 minutes

NUTRITIONAL INFO PER SERVING:

Calories 287; Carbs 3.3g; Net Carbs 1.2g; Fiber 0.8; Protein 12g; Fat 23g;

INGREDIENTS:

2 LARGE EGGS

½ LB SLICED LIVER

SALT AND PEPPER, TO TASTE

1 TBSP BUTTER

½ TBSP BLACK TRUFFLE OIL

1 TBSP CREAM

DIRECTIONS:

1. Preheat the Air Fryer to 340° F.
2. Cut the liver into thin slices and put in the fridge.
3. Separate whites the yolks, and put each yolk in a cup.
4. In another bowl, add the cream, the truffle oil, salt, and pepper and beat the combined mixture with a fork.
5. Take the liver and arrange ½ of the mixture in a small ramekin.
6. Pour the white of the egg and divide it equally between ramekins.
7. Put the yolks on top.
8. Surround each yolk with the liver and cook for 12 minutes. Serve cold.

Eggplant Caviar

Servings: 3

Prep + Cook Time: 20 minutes

NUTRITIONAL INFO PER SERVING:

Calories 287; Carbs 18.3g; Net Carbs 5.2g; Fiber 13.2g; Protein 4g; Fat 7g

INGREDIENTS:

2 MEDIUM EGGPLANTS

½ RED ONION

1½ TBSP BALSAMIC VINEGAR

1 TBSP OLIVE OIL

DIRECTIONS:

1. Preheat the Air Fryer. Wash, then dry the eggplants.
2. Arrange them in a plate and cook them for 20 minutes at 360° F.
3. Remove the eggplants from the oven and let them cool down.
4. Blend the onion in a blender.
5. Cut the eggplants in half, lengthwise, and empty their insides with a spoon.
6. Put the inside of the eggplants in the mixer and process everything.
7. Add the vinegar, the olive oil and a little bit of salt, then blend again.
8. Serve cool with tomato sauce or ketchup.

Cheesy Homemade Broccoli

Servings: 3

Prep + Cook Time: 20 minutes

NUTRITIONAL INFO PER SERVING:

Calories 432; Carbs 8.3g; Net Carbs 3.2g; Fiber 5.2g; Protein 24g; Fat 37g

INGREDIENTS:

1 LB BROCCOLI

4 EGGS

1 CUP CREAM

A PINCH OF NUTMEG

1 TBSP GINGER POWDER

1 CUP SHREDDED CHEESE

SALT AND PEPPER, TO TASTE

DIRECTIONS:

1. Cook the broccoli on steam for around 4 minutes.
2. Drain the broccoli and combine with one egg and the cream.
3. Add the nutmeg, the ginger, salt, and pepper.
4. Butter several small ramekins and spread the mixture.
5. Sprinkle cheese on top. Set the timer to 20 minutes and cook at 220°F.

Pin Wheel

Servings: 4

Prep + Cook Time: 6 minutes

NUTRITIONAL INFO PER SERVING:

Calories 392; Carbs 9.3g; Net Carbs 3.2g; Fiber 3.2g; Protein 15g; Fat 35g

INGREDIENTS:

2 LB DILL PICKLES

1 LB SOFTENED CREAM CHEESE

3 OZ SLICED HAM

2 ALMOND TORTILLAS

SALT AND BLACK PEPPER, TO TASTE

DIRECTIONS:

1. Spread the cream cheese on one side of the tortilla. Put a slice of ham over it. Spread a layer of cheese on top of the ham.

2. Roll 1 pickle up in the tortilla. Preheat the Air Fryer to 340° F.

3. Place the rolls in the basket of the Air Fryer and cook for 6 minutes.

Main Dishes

Crunchy Chicken Fingers

Servings: 2

Prep + Cook Time: 8 minutes

NUTRITIONAL INFO PER SERVING:

Calories 132; Carbs 1.1g; Net Carbs 0.7g; Fiber 0.1g; Protein 18g; Fat 4

INGREDIENTS:

¼ TSP FRESH CHOPPED CHIVES

1 TBSP PARMESAN CHEESE

¼ TSP FRESH CHOPPED THYME

¼ TSP BLACK PEPPER

½ CUP PORK RINDS

1 EGG WHITE

1 TSP WATER

5 OZ BONELESS AND SKINLESS CHICKEN BREAST, CUT INTO FINGERS

DIRECTIONS:

1. Preheat the Air Fryer to 390° F, if needed.
2. Mix the chives, the Parmesan, the thyme, the pepper, and the rinds.
3. Whisk and mix the egg white and the water.
4. Cut the chicken breasts in large strips.
5. Carefully dip chicken strips into egg mixture and pork rinds mixture.
6. Place the strips one by one in the air fryer basket. Cook for 8 minutes.

Spicy Chicken Wings

Servings: 2

Prep + Cook Time: 23 minutes

NUTRITIONAL INFO PER SERVING:

Calories 235; Carbs 1.3g; Net Carbs 1g; Fiber 0.3g; Protein 37g; Fat 7g

INGREDIENTS:

1 ½ TBSP HOT CHILI SAUCE

½ TBSP LIQUID STEVIA

¼ TBSP THE LIME JUICE OF 1 LIME

12 OZ CHICKEN WINGS

KOSHER SALT AND BLACK GROUND FRESH PEPPER TO TASTE

DIRECTIONS:

1. Preheat the Air Fryer to 390° F, if needed. Mix the lime juice, the stevia, and the chili sauce.

2. Toss the chicken wings with the lime and the chili sauce mixture.

3. Put the chicken wings in the Air Fryer basket and cook for around 20 minutes. Shake the basket every 4 to 5 minutes. Serve hot.

Lime Bacon Shrimp

Servings: 16

Prep + Cook Time: 10 minutes

NUTRITIONAL INFO PER SERVING:

Calories 125; Carbs 2g; Net Carbs 1.2g; Fiber 0.8g; Protein 11g; Fat 10g

INGREDIENTS:

1 ¼ LBS SHRIMP, PEELED, 16 PIECES

1 LB BACON, 16 SLICES

JUICE FROM 1 LEMON

DIRECTIONS:

1. Take a slice of bacon and carefully wrap it around one shrimp, starting from the shrimp's head.
2. Put the wrapped shrimps into the fridge for 25 minutes.
3. Preheat the air fryer to 390°F, if needed.
4. Cook them for 6 – 8 minutes. Sprinkle with lemon juice and serve.

Korean Barbecued Satay

Servings: 3

Prep + Cook Time: 15 minutes

NUTRITIONAL INFO PER SERVING:

Calories 434; Carbs 11.3g; Net Carbs 6.8g; Fiber 2.1g; Protein 29g; Fat 31g

INGREDIENTS:

12 OZ BONELESS AND SKINLESS CHICKEN TENDERS

½ CUP SOY SAUCE

¼ CUP SESAME OIL

4 CHOPPED CLOVES GARLIC

4 CHOPPED SCALLIONS

1 TBSP FRESH GRATED GINGER

2 TBSP TOASTED SESAME SEEDS

A PINCH OF BLACK PEPPER

DIRECTIONS:

1. Start by skewering each tender and trim any excess fat.
2. Mix the rest of the ingredients in one large bowl.
3. Add the skewered chicken and place them in the fridge for a period of 4 to 24 hours. Preheat the Air Fryer to 390°F, if needed.
4. Pat the chicken until it is completely dry using paper towel.
5. Cook for 7-10 minutes.

Portobello Mushroom Melts

Servings: 2

Prep + Cook Time: 25 minutes

NUTRITIONAL INFO PER SERVING:

Calories 243; Carbs 8.3g; Net Carbs 2g; Fiber 2.2g; Protein 13g; Fat 16g

INGREDIENTS:

1 TBSP OLIVE OIL

1 TSP BALSAMIC VINEGAR

1 OZ STEMMED AND SLICED MUSHROOMS

¼ LARGE RED ONION

SEA SALT AND BLACK PEPPER

3 FLAXSEED TORTILLAS

2 OZ CREAM CHEESE

2 TBSP PESTO SAUCE

½ TOMATO

2 OZ MOZZARELLA CHEESE

DIRECTIONS:

1. Preheat the Air Fryer to 390° F, if needed.
2. Mix olive oil and balsamic vinegar. Add the mushrooms and the onion.
3. Season with salt and black pepper. Cook for 5 minutes.
4. Remove them from the fryer, then lower the temperature to 330° F.
5. Brush each side of the tortillas with olive oil.
6. Top the tortillas with cream cheese, mushrooms and onions.
7. Spread the pesto on the tortillas and press against the mushrooms.
8. Top with tomato, cheese and cook for 7 minutes until the cheese melts.

Pepperoni Portobello

Servings: 3

Prep + Cook Time: 9 minutes

NUTRITIONAL INFO PER SERVING:

Calories 340; Carbs 7.3g; Net Carbs 3.8g; Fiber 3.2g; Protein 37g; Fat 19g

INGREDIENTS:

3 PORTOBELLO MUSHROOMS

3 TBSP OLIVE OIL

3 TBSP TOMATO SAUCE

3 TBSP SHREDDED MOZZARELLA

12 SLICES PEPPERONI

A PINCH OF SALT

A PINCH OF DRIED ITALIAN SEASONINGS

DIRECTIONS:

1. Preheat the air fryer to 330°F, if needed.
2. Drizzle a little bit of olive oil on each side of the mushroom.
3. Season the inside of each mushroom with salt and Italian seasonings.
4. Spread tomato sauce evenly over the mushrooms and top with cheese.
5. Place the stuffed mushrooms in the cooking basket and insert in the air fryer.
6. After just 1 minute, remove the basket from the air fryer and add the pepperoni slices on top of the portobello pizza.
7. Place back on fire and cook for 4 to 5 more minutes.
8. Finish the dish by topping the pizza with grated Parmesan cheese and flakes of crushed red pepper.

Yummy Meatballs in Tomato Sauce

Servings: 3

Prep + Cook Time: 23 minutes

NUTRITIONAL INFO PER SERVING:

Calories 441; Carbs 6.3g; Net Carbs 3.2g; Fiber 2.2g; Protein 22g; Fat 37g

INGREDIENTS:

1 MEDIUM ONION

12 OZ GROUND BEEF MEAT

1 TBSP FRESH CHOPPED PARSLEY

½ TBSP CHOPPED THYME LEAVES

1 EGG

3 TBSP PORK RINDS

SALT AND PEPPER, TO TASTE

6 OZ TOMATO SAUCE

DIRECTIONS:

1. Place the ingredients into a bowl and mix very well.
2. Step by step, shape the mixture into 10 to 12 balls.
3. Preheat the Air Fryer to 390° F, if needed.
4. Place the meatballs in the air fryer basket, and cook for 8-9 minutes.
5. Remove the meatballs and transfer to an oven plate.
6. Add in the tomato sauce and place in the Air Fryer.
7. Cook again at 330° F for 4 minutes.

Salmon with Dill Sauce

Servings: 2

Prep + Cook Time: 28 minutes

NUTRITIONAL INFO PER SERVING:

Calories 291; Carbs 7.4g; Net Carbs 5.6g; Fiber 0.2g; Protein 15g; Fat 23g

INGREDIENTS:

2 PIECES SALMON, 6 OZ EACH

2 TBSP OLIVE OIL

A PINCH OF SALT

FOR THE DILL SAUCE:

½ CUP FULL-FAT GREEK YOGURT

½ CUP SOUR CREAM

A PINCH OF SALT

2 TBSP FINELY CHOPPED DILL

DIRECTIONS:

1. Preheat the Air Fryer to 270°F.
2. Cut the salmon into four equal sized portions then drizzle with oil.
3. Season with a pinch of sea salt.
4. Place the seasoned salmon into the Air Fryer's cooking basket.
5. Cook for 20-25 minutes and top with dill sauce.
6. For the dill sauce: in a large mixing bowl, combine the yogurt, the sour cream, the chopped dill, and salt.
7. Beat well until smooth.

Tomato Galette

Servings: 3

Prep + Cook Time: 5 minutes

NUTRITIONAL INFO PER SERVING:

Calories 131; Carbs 7.3g; Net Carbs 2g; Fiber 3.1g; Protein 13g; Fat 5g

INGREDIENTS:

3 LARGE TOMATOES

A PINCH OF SALT

A PINCH OF BLACK PEPPER

2 TBSP HERBS

1 TBSP OLIVE OIL

1 CUP MOZZARELLA CHEESE

DIRECTIONS:

1. Cut the tomatoes in half and arranges them in the Air Fryer.
2. Sprinkle with ground black pepper and salt.
3. Add dried herbs of your choice.
4. Top with cheese.
5. Add parsley, basil, oregano, thyme, rosemary, and sage.
6. Make sure that you have placed the tomatoes face up.
7. Set the timer to 20 minutes and the heat to 320° F.
8. Serve warm and enjoy!

Persian Mushrooms

Servings: 4

Prep + Cook Time: 20 minutes

NUTRITIONAL INFO PER SERVING:

Calories 240; Carbs 9.3g; Net Carbs 7.2g; Fiber 0.5g; Protein 10g; Fat 19g

INGREDIENTS:

6 PORTOBELLO MUSHROOMS

3 OZ SOFTENED BUTTER

2 LARGE SHALLOTS

2 CLOVES GARLIC

1 TBSP FRESH PARSLEY

A PINCH OF SALT

A PINCH OF PEPPER

1 CUP GRATED PARMESAN

DIRECTIONS:

1. Preheat the Air Fryer to 390° F, if needed.
2. Clean the mushrooms and remove the stems.
3. Slice the shallots and the garlic.
4. Now, place the mushroom stems, the garlic and the shallots, the parsley and the softened butter in a blender.
5. Arrange the caps of the mushrooms in the basket of the Air Fryer.
6. Stuff the caps with the mixture and sprinkle with Parmesan cheese.
7. Set the timer to 20 minutes.

Chili Rellenos

Servings: 5

Prep + Cook Time: 35 minutes

NUTRITIONAL INFO PER SERVING:

Calories 258; Carbs 4.8g; Net Carbs 2g; Fiber 2.2g; Protein 15g; Fat 20g

INGREDIENTS:

2 CANS GREEN CHILI PEPPERS

1 CUP MONTEREY JACK CHEESE.

1 CUP SHREDDED CHEDDAR CHEESE

2 LARGE AND BEATEN EGGS

½ CUP WATER

2 TBSP ALMOND FLOUR

½ CUP MILK

1 CAN TOMATO SAUCE

DIRECTIONS:

1. Preheat the Air Fryer to 350 °F, if needed.
2. Spray a baking dish with the cooking spray.
3. Take half of the chilies and arrange them in the baking dish.
4. Top chilies with half of the cheese and cover with the remaining chilies.
5. In a medium bowl, combine the eggs, the water, the flour.
6. Pour the mixture over the chilies. Fry for 25 minutes.
7. Remove the chilies from the Air Fryer, and pour the tomato sauce over.
8. Cook again for 10 minutes.
9. Top with the remaining cheese, to serve.

Cajun Sautéed Shrimp

Servings: 4

Prep + Cook Time: 8 minutes

NUTRITIONAL INFO PER SERVING:

Calories 73; Carbs 0.8g; Net Carbs 0.6g; Fiber 0.2g; Protein 6g; Fat 4g

INGREDIENTS:

4 OZ TIGER SHRIMP, 16 TO 20

¼ A TBSP CAYENNE PEPPER

½ A TBSP OLD BAY SEASONING

¼ A TBSP SMOKED PAPRIKA

A PINCH OF SEA SALT

1 TBSP OLIVE OIL

DIRECTIONS:

1. Preheat the Air Fryer to 390°F, if needed. In a large mixing bowl, put the ingredients. Coat the shrimps with a little bit of oil and spices.

2. Gently place the shrimp in the cooking basket and cook for 5 minutes.

Chicken Dishes

Air Fried Chicken Legs

Servings: 4

Prep + Cook Time: 50 minutes

NUTRITIONAL INFO PER SERVING:

Calories 483; Carbs 4.8g; Net Carbs 2.6g; Fiber 1.6g; Protein 49g; Fat 27g

INGREDIENTS:

4 QUARTERS CHICKEN LEGS

¼ CUP OLIVE OIL

3 LARGE HALVED LEMONS

4 TBSP DRIED OREGANO

4 TBSP DRIED BASIL.

4 TBSP GARLIC POWDER

SALT AND BLACK PEPPER, TO TASTE

DIRECTIONS:

1. Preheat the Air Fryer to 350° F, if needed.
2. Place the chicken legs in a deep bowl.
3. Brush the chicken legs with a tbsp. of extra virgin olive oil.
4. Squeeze lemon juice over the chicken and arrange in the fryer's rack.
5. Place the lemons around the chicken.
6. In a medium bowl, combine oregano, basil, garlic, salt, and pepper.
7. Sprinkle the mixture on the chicken legs.
8. Cook the chicken in the preheated Air Fryer for 60 minutes.

Tarragon Chicken Breast

Servings: 2

Prep + Cook Time: 13 minutes

NUTRITIONAL INFO PER SERVING:

Calories 187; Carbs 0.5g; Net Carbs 0.3g; Fiber 0.1g; Protein 31g; Fat 5g

INGREDIENTS:

2 BONELESS AND SKINLESS CHICKEN BREASTS

¼ CUP DRIED TARRAGON

½ TBSP UNSALTED BUTTER

¼ TSP KOSHER SALT

¼ TSP BLACK AND FRESH GROUND PEPPER

DIRECTIONS:

1. Preheat the Air Fryer to 390° F, if needed.
2. Place each of the chicken breasts on a foil wrap, 12x12 inches.
3. Top the chicken with the tarragon sprig and the butter.
4. Season with salt and pepper.
5. Wrap the foil around the chicken breast in a loose way, so there is a flow of air.
6. Cook the foil wrapped chicken in the Air Fryer for 13 minutes.
7. Slowly and carefully unwrap the chicken and serve hot.

Chicken Adobo

Servings: 2

Prep + Cook Time: 15 minutes

NUTRITIONAL INFO PER SERVING:

Calories 419; Carbs 11.1g; Net Carbs 5.1g; Fiber 3.2g; Protein 34g; Fat 19g

INGREDIENTS:

2 BONELESS AND SKINLESS CHICKEN BREASTS

2 TBSP LIME JUICE

1 TBSP MINCED FRESH CILANTRO

1 TBSP OLIVE OIL

3 MINCED GARLIC CLOVES

1 MINCED GREEN ONION

¼ TBSP GROUND CUMIN

¼ TBSP MINCED FRESH THYME

¼ TBSP MINCED FRESH OREGANO

SALT AND PEPPER, TO TASTE

DIRECTIONS:

1. Mix the ingredients in a resealable plastic bag and seal the bag.
2. Refrigerate for at least 3 hours.
3. Then drain the marinade.
4. Using long tongs, moist paper toweling with the oil and coat the Air Fryer's rack.
5. Set the heat to 340°F and time to 20 minutes.
6. Don't forget to flip the chicken at least once in the cooking process.

Chicken Cordon Bleu

Servings: 4

Prep + Cook Time: 35 minutes

NUTRITIONAL INFO PER SERVING:

Calories 564; Carbs 5g; Net Carbs 2.2g; Fiber 0.8g; Protein 48g; Fat 52g

INGREDIENTS:

4 SKINLESS AND BONELESS CHICKEN BREASTS

4 SLICES SWISS CHEESE

4 SLICES HAM

3 TBSP ALMOND FLOUR

1 TBSP PAPRIKA

4 TBSP BUTTER

½ CUP DRY WHITE WINE

1 TBSP CHICKEN BOUILLON GRANULES

1 CUP HEAVY WHIPPING CREAM

DIRECTIONS:

1. Preheat the Air Fryer to 390° F, if needed.
2. Pound the chicken breasts and put a slice of ham on each of the chicken breasts.
3. Fold the edges of the chicken over the filling and secure the sides with toothpicks.
4. In a medium bowl, combine flour and paprika and coat the chicken pieces. Set the timer to 15 minutes and cook the chicken.
5. In a large skillet, heat the butter and add the bouillon and the wine.
6. Reduce the heat to low. Remove the chicken from the Air Fryer and add it to the skillet.
7. Let the ingredients simmer for around 30 minutes and serve.

Chinese-Style Marinated Chicken

Servings: 6

Prep + Cook Time: 20 minutes

NUTRITIONAL INFO PER SERVING:

Calories 523; Carbs 4g; Net Carbs 2.5g; Fiber 0.5g; Protein 31g; Fat 46g

INGREDIENTS:

2 LBS CHICKEN BREASTS, CUT INTO CUBES

¼ CUP PORK RINDS

2 LARGE EGGS

6 TBSP ALMOND FLOUR

1 TBSP BAKING POWDER

½ CUP VEGETABLE OIL

4 TBSP SESAME OIL

2 TBSP GRATED AND FRESH GINGER ROOTS

½ CUP CHOPPED GREEN ONION

½ CUP WATER

¼ CUP WHITE VINEGAR

1 ½ TBSP LIQUID STEVIA

2 TBSP SOY SAUCE

¼ CUP OYSTER SAUCE

DIRECTIONS:

1. Preheat the Air Fryer to 390° F, if needed. Coat the chicken cubes with the pork rinds, then set aside.

2. In a large bowl, beat eggs, salt, and pepper until the mixture is smooth.

3. Add flour and baking powder, and beat until there are no lumps. Coat the chicken and place it on the rack of the Air Fryer. Pour 2 tablespoons of oil and cook it for 15 minutes. Remove and set aside.

4. In a skillet, heat oil. Then stir in sesame oil, onion, and ginger. Cook and keep stirring for 2-3 minutes.

5. Add the water, the vinegar, the stevia and boil the mixture. In soy sauce, dissolve pork rinds, and add vinegar and oyster sauce.

6. Keep stirring until the sauce thickens. Add the chicken and let simmer for 10-15 minutes.

Chicken Marsala

Servings: 4

Prep + Cook Time: 30 minutes

NUTRITIONAL INFO PER SERVING:

Calories 488; Carbs 5g; Net Carbs 3.2g; Fiber 0.9g; Protein 37g; Fat 43g

INGREDIENTS:

¼ CUP ALMOND FLOUR

½ TBSP DRIED OREGANO

4 SKINLESS AND BONELESS CHICKEN BREASTS

4 TBSP BUTTER

4 TBSP OLIVE OIL

1 CUP SLICED MUSHROOMS

½ CUP MARSALA WINE

SALT AND BLACK PEPPER, TO TASTE

¼ CUP COOKING SHERRY

DIRECTIONS:

1. Preheat the Air Fryer to 350° F, if needed.

2. In a bowl, combine the flour, the salt, the pepper, and the oregano.

3. Coat the chicken with flour and arrange it on the rack of the Air Fryer.

4. Pour over one tablespoon of oil and cook for 12 minutes.

5. After that, add the mushrooms and cook for 5 more minutes.

6. Transfer the ingredients to a pan and pour wine and sherry.

7. Let simmer for 10 minutes.

Greek Chicken

Servings: 5

Prep + Cook Time: 50 minutes

NUTRITIONAL INFO PER SERVING:

Calories 398; Carbs 3g; Net Carbs 2.1g; Fiber 0.4g; Protein 33g; Fat 28g

INGREDIENTS:

2 LB CHICKEN, CUT IN PIECES

½ CUP OLIVE OIL

3 CHOPPED CLOVES GARLIC

1 TBSP FRESH ROSEMARY

1 TBSP FRESH THYME

1 TBSP CHOPPED FRESH OREGANO

2 LARGE LEMON

½ CUP WHITE WINE

SALT AND BLACK PEPPER, TO TASTE

DIRECTIONS:

1. In a large bowl, combine garlic, prunes, olives, capers, olive oil, vinegar, bay leaves, oregano, salt, and pepper.

2. Mix the ingredients very well.

3. Spread the mixture into a baking dish.

4. Add the chicken. Keep stirring.

5. Preheat the Air Fryer to 350° F and place in the chicken.

6. Sprinkle with white wine and cook it for 50 minutes.

Asian Chicken

Servings: 3

Prep + Cook Time: 40 minutes

NUTRITIONAL INFO PER SERVING:

Calories 243; Carbs 11.3g; Net Carbs 6.1g; Fiber 4.2g; Protein 18g; Fat 13g

INGREDIENTS:

3 CLOVES GARLIC

½ LB CHICKEN

1 TBSP CUMIN POWDER

1 LARGE ONION

2 TBSP OIL

1 TBSP MUSTARD

3 GREEN CHILI PEPPERS

A PINCH OF GINGER

A PINCH OF FRESH AND CHOPPED CORIANDER

2 TOMATOES

SALT AND BLACK PEPPER, TO TASTE

DIRECTIONS:

1. Start by heating the oil in a deep pan.
2. Add mustard, cumin, onion, ginger, and the green peppers.
3. Sauté the mixture for a few minutes.
4. Add tomatoes, coriander, cumin powder, and salt, and keep stirring.
5. Preheat the Air Fryer to 360° F.
6. Coat the chicken with oil, salt, and pepper and cook it for 30 minutes.
7. Remove it from the Air Fryer and pour the sauce over and around it.

Chicken Noodles

Servings: 4

Prep + Cook Time: 30 minutes |

NUTRITIONAL INFO PER SERVING:

Calories 523; Carbs 3g; Net Carbs 1.8g; Fiber 0.6g; Protein 41g; Fat 34g

INGREDIENTS:

4 CHICKEN BREASTS, SKINLESS AND BONELESS

SALT AND BLACK PEPPER

1 TBSP ROSEMARY

1 TBSP TOMATO PASTE

1 TBSP RED PEPPER

1 TBSP ALL SPICES

FOR THE NOODLES:

2 CUPS ALMOND FLOUR

½ TBSP SALT

2 BEATEN EGGS

DIRECTIONS:

1. Preheat the Air Fryer to 350° F, if needed. Coat the chicken with 1 tbsp of butter, salt, and pepper. Arrange the chicken breasts in the basket and cook for 20 minutes.

2. For the noodles, combine flour, salt, and egg, and make a dough. Place the dough on a floured surface. Knead and cover it. Set aside for 30 minutes.

3. Roll the dough on a floured surface. When the batter thins, cut it into thin strips and let it dry for 1 hour.

4. Meanwhile, take the chicken out of the Air Fryer and put it aside. Boil the chicken broth and add noodles, tomato paste, and red pepper. Cook for 5 minutes. Add the spices and stir in the noodles. Salt and pepper to taste.

5. Serve the noodles with the air fried chicken.

Pepper Chicken Tenders

Servings: 20

Prep + Cook Time: 15 minutes

NUTRITIONAL INFO PER SERVING:

Calories 54; Carbs o.4g; Net Carbs 0.2g; Fiber 0.2g; Protein 6g; Fat 3g

INGREDIENTS:

1.5 LB CHICKEN TENDERS

20 SKEWERS BAMBOO PARTY

2 ZESTED LEMONS

3 TBSP EXTRA VIRGIN OLIVE OIL

SALT AND BLACK PEPPER

DIRECTIONS:

1. Preheat the Air Fryer to 350° F, if needed.
2. Season the chicken pieces with salt and black pepper.
3. Thread the pieces onto skewers.
4. In a dish, mix lemon juice and olive oil.
5. Coat the chicken tenders and cook the chicken tenders in the preheated Air Fryer for about 12 minutes.
6. Serve with tomato sauce and fried chips.

Steaks

Baby Back Ribs

Servings: 4

Prep + Cook Time: 30 minutes

NUTRITIONAL INFO PER SERVING:

Calories 631; Carbs 5g; Net Carbs 2.9g; Fiber 0.5g; Protein 57g; Fat 67g

INGREDIENTS:

1 SLAB BABY BACK RIBS

1 TBSP GRATED GINGER

1 MINCED SCALLION

½ TBSP CHOPPED CILANTRO

1 SMALL SEEDED AND CHOPPED JALAPEÑO

1 MINCED CLOVE GARLIC

½ CUP ORANGE JUICE

2 TBSP SESAME OIL

DIRECTIONS:

1. Put the ingredients inside a plastic bag overnight.
2. Reserve the marinade.
3. Place the ribs vertically in the Air Fryer.
4. Cook for 30 minutes at 365° F.
5. Meanwhile, put the marinade in a deep cooking pan.
6. Cook the marinade on medium heat for 5 minutes.
7. Brush the ribs with the marinade.

Roasted Lamb with Pumpkin

Servings: 2

Prep + Cook Time: 35 minutes

NUTRITIONAL INFO PER SERVING:

Calories 587; Carbs 8.1g; Net Carbs 3.2g; Fiber 2.3g; Protein 46g; Fat 39g

INGREDIENTS:

1 LB LAMB RACK

1 TBSP DIJON MUSTARD

2 OZ PORK RINDS

2 TBSP CHOPPED FRESH HERBS

1 OZ GRATED PARMESAN

1 LEMON ZEST

1 TBSP OLIVE OIL.

1 MEDIUM PUMPKIN

1 TBSP OLIVE OIL

SALT AND PEPPER, TO TASTE

DIRECTIONS:

1. Preheat the Air Fryer to 390° F for 3 minutes. Pat the lamb dry using a towel. Remove the fat and rub the meat with mustard.

2. Blitz the rinds with herbs, Parmesan, lemon zest and the seasonings.

3. Season the joint. Place the meat in the Air Fryer and drizzle with oil.

4. Roast the meat for around 15 minutes.

5. For the wedges, start by peeling and coring the pumpkin; then coat it with oil. Season the pumpkin and place it aside.

6. Remove lamb from the Air Fryer and place it on a serving dish.

7. Place the pumpkin wedges in the Air Fryer and roast for 18 minutes.

8. Once ready, serve the meat with the salad and the wedges!

Beef Fajitas

Servings: 4

Prep + Cook Time: 15 minutes

NUTRITIONAL INFO PER SERVING:

Calories 567; Carbs 7.3g; Net Carbs 2.1g; Fiber 5.2g; Protein 41g; Fat 46g

INGREDIENTS:

2 LB BEEF, CUT INTO THIN STRIPS

6 TBSP COCONUT OIL

½ CUP LEMON OR LIME JUICE

4 PEELED AND MASHED GARLIC CLOVES

½ TBSP CHILI POWDER

1 RED PEPPER

1 SLICED PEPPER

2 SLICED ONIONS

12 FLAXSEED TORTILLAS

2 TBSP MELTED BUTTER

1 AVOCADO

DIRECTIONS:

1. Prepare a combination of oil and lime juice.
2. Add the spices and the beef and mix the ingredients very well.
3. Marinate for 5 hours.
4. Remove the marinated mixture from the fridge and pat dry the meat.
5. Take the basket of the Air Fryer and arrange the meat portions inside.
6. Pour 2 tbsp. of olive oil over the meat.
7. Set the timer to 35 minutes and the heat to 360° F.
8. In the meantime, sauté the vegetables in the coconut oil and then add them to the Air Fryer.

9. Heat the tortillas for a short time in a non-stick pan and brush them with melted butter.

10.   Serve the beef meat with the tortillas and enjoy this delicious taste!

Stuffed Pork Chops

Servings: 3

Prep + Cook Time: 40 minutes

NUTRITIONAL INFO PER SERVING:

Calories 412; Carbs 1.5g; Net Carbs 1.2g; Fiber 0.6g; Protein 28g; Fat 28g

INGREDIENTS:

3 THICK PORK CHOPS

A PINCH OF HERBS

7 CHOPPED MUSHROOMS

1 TBSP ALMOND FLOUR

1 TBSP LEMON JUICE

SALT AND BLACK PEPPER, TO TASTE

DIRECTIONS:

1. Preheat the Air Fryer to 350°F, if needed.

2. Season each side of the meat with the salt and pepper.

3. Arrange the chops in the Air Fryer and cook for 15 minutes at 350°F.

4. Meanwhile, cook the mushroom for 3 minutes, in a skillet, and stir in the lemon juice. Add the flour and then mix the herbs.

5. Cook the mixture for 4 minutes. Then set aside.

6. Cut five pieces of foil for each of the chops. On every piece of foil put a chop in the middle and cover it with the mushroom mixture.

7. Now, carefully fold the foil and seal around the chop.

8. Put the chops in the Air Fryer for 30 minutes. Serve with salad.

Ground Beef Kebab Skewers

Servings: 2

Prep + Cook Time: 25 minutes

NUTRITIONAL INFO PER SERVING:

Calories 331; Carbs 5g; Net Carbs 2.5g; Fiber 1.6g; Protein 33g; Fat 22g

INGREDIENTS:

½ LB GROUND BEEF

½ LARGE ONION

1 MEDIUM GREEN CHILI

½ TBSP CHILI POWDER

1 MINCED CLOVE GARLIC

A PINCH OF GINGER

1 TBSP GARAM MASALA

3 TBSP PORK RINDS

DIRECTIONS:

1. Grate 1 pinch of ginger and the garlic. Chop and deseed the chili.
2. Chop the onion. Mix ginger, garlic, chili and onion with ground beef.
3. Add the powdered spices. Add a few pork rinds and salt.
4. Shape the beef into fat sausages around short wooden skewers.
5. Set the skewers aside for 1 hour, then cook them in a preheated Air Fryer for 25 minutes at 350° F.

Lamb Rib Saltimbocca

Servings: 4

Prep + Cook Time: 20 minutes

NUTRITIONAL INFO PER SERVING:

Calories 623; Carbs 5g; Net Carbs 3.2g; Fiber 1.2g; Protein 63g; Fat 38g

INGREDIENTS:

2 LBS LAMB RACKS, CUT INTO QUARTERS

2 BALLS MOZZARELLA

4 LEAVES SAGE

4 SLICES THIN PROSCIUTTO

2 TBSP OLIVE OIL

DIRECTIONS:

1. Preheat the Air Fryer to 350°F, if needed. Make a deep pocket in each of the lamb chops. Stuff the pockets with sliced mozzarella cheese.

2. Put a sage leaf on the top of every chop. Wrap each chop with a slice of prosciutto. Pour 1 tbsp. of olive oil on the lamb and cook it for 15 minutes.

3. Remove the meat from the Air Fryer and transfer to a serving dish.

Salt and Pepper Beef Ribs

Servings: 6

Prep + Cook Time: 65 minutes

NUTRITIONAL INFO PER SERVING:

Calories 561; Carbs 6g; Net Carbs 3.15g; Fiber 2.1g; Protein 28g; Fat 53g

INGREDIENTS:

2 RACKS BEEF RIBS

2 TBSP FRESHLY GROUND GINGER.

2 TSP BLACK PEPPER

1 TBSP SALT

5 DROPS LIQUID STEVIA

1 TBSP SPANISH PAPRIKA

DIRECTIONS:

1. Mix the seasonings very well. Coat each side of the beef ribs. Arrange the ribs in a preheated Air Fryer basket.

2. Set the heat to 390° F and the timer to 55 minutes. Top with the seasonings.

Asian Liver Curry

Servings: 2

Prep + Cook Time: 18 minutes

NUTRITIONAL INFO PER SERVING:

Calories 212; Carbs 13.3g; Net Carbs 7.5g; Fiber 4.2g; Protein 26g; Fat 7g

INGREDIENTS:

½ LB BEEF LIVER

1 SLICED ONION

1 LARGE TOMATO

1 MINCED CLOVE GARLIC

1 TBSP GINGER

1 TBSP PAPRIKA

½ TBSP CHILI POWDER

1 TBSP CUMIN POWDER

½ TBSP GROUND CORIANDER

½ TBSP TURMERIC

½ TBSP GARAM MASALA

4 DROPS LIQUID STEVIA

CORIANDER LEAVES

DIRECTIONS:

1. In a skillet, fry the onion on medium heat until it tenders.
2. Now, add the grated ginger and the garlic. Keep stirring.
3. Add the powdered spices, then fry for 3 more minutes.
4. Meanwhile, season the liver with salt and pepper.
5. Place the liver in the Air Fryer and cook it for 15 minutes at 350° F.
6. Remove the liver from the Air Fryer and transfer it to the skillet.
7. Add the chopped tomato, the stevia and a little bit of water until everything is cooked. Garnish with coriander.

Fish and Seafood

Cedar Planked Salmon

Servings: 6

Prep + Cook Time: 35 minutes |

NUTRITIONAL INFO PER SERVING:

Calories 476; Carbs 6.3g; Net Carbs 4.1g; Fiber 0.8g; Protein 33g; Fat 38g

INGREDIENTS:

4 UNTREATED CEDAR PLANKS

½ CUP VEGETABLE OIL

1½ TBSP RICE VINEGAR

1 TBSP SESAME OIL

½ CUP SOY SAUCE

¼ CUP LARGE AND CHOPPED GREEN ONIONS

1 TBSP GRATED AND FRESH GINGER ROOT

1 TBSP MINCED GARLIC

2 LB SALMON FILLETS, SKIN REMOVED

DIRECTIONS:

1. Start by soaking the cedar planks for 2 hours.
2. Take a shallow dish and stir in the vegetable oil, the rice vinegar, the sesame oil, the soy sauce, the green onions, and ginger.
3. Put the salmon fillets in the prepared marinade for at least 20 minutes.
4. Place the planks in the basket of the Air Fryer.
5. Cook the salmon fillets for around 15 minutes at 360°F.

Coconut Fried Shrimp

Servings: 4

Prep + Cook Time: 15 minutes

NUTRITIONAL INFO PER SERVING:

Calories 156; Carbs 6.5g; Net Carbs 3.2g; Fiber 2.2g; Protein 17g; Fat 2g

INGREDIENTS:

½ CUP WATER

½ TBSP BAKING POWDER

1 TBSP SALT

½ CUP ALMOND FLOUR

½ TBSP RED PEPPER FLAKES

4 TBSP RICE WINE VINEGAR

½ CUP STRAWBERRY MARMALADE

2 CUPS SHREDDED SWEETENED COCONUTS

½ CUP PORK RINDS

1 LB LARGE PEELED AND DEVEINED SHRIMP

DIRECTIONS:

1. For the dipping sauce: add red pepper flakes, vinegar, and marmalade to a saucepan. Heat around 10 minutes on low heat.
2. Keep stirring until the mixture is combined.
3. Now, in a deep bowl, whisk the salt, the flour, and the baking powder.
4. Add water. Whisk everything until the mixture becomes smooth.
5. Set the batter aside for 15 minutes.
6. In another bowl, toss the coconut and pork rinds.
7. Dip each shrimp into batter and then coat it with coconut mixture.
8. Set the heat to 390° F and fry them for 3 minutes.
9. Serve the shrimps with the dipping sauce.

Pomfret Fish Fry

Servings: 5

Prep + Cook Time: 15 minutes

NUTRITIONAL INFO PER SERVING:

Calories 463; Carbs 10.3g; Net Carbs 3.4g; Fiber 3.2g; Protein 55g; Fat 23g

INGREDIENTS:

4 ONIONS

3 LB SILVER POMFRET

1 TBSP TURMERIC POWDER

3 PINCHES OF RED CHILI POWDER

¾ TBSP GINGER

3 PINCHES OF CUMIN POWDER

2 TBSP LEMON JUICE

2 TBSP OLIVE OIL

SALT AND BLACK PEPPER, TO TASTE

DIRECTIONS:

1. Wash the fish and soak in lemon juice to remove any unpleasant smell.

2. After 30 minutes, remove and wash the fish.

3. Draw diagonal shaped slits on the fish. Combine black pepper, salt, garlic paste, lemon juice, and the turmeric powder.

4. Rub the mixture above and inside the fish and refrigerate for 30 minutes to absorb the seasoning.

5. Arrange the fish in the basket of the Air Fryer and pour 2 tbsp. of oil. Cook it for 12 minutes at 340° F.

Salmon Quiche

Servings: 4

Prep + Cook Time: 8 minutes

NUTRITIONAL INFO PER SERVING:

Calories 515; Carbs 4.3g; Net Carbs 2.6g; Fiber 0.8g; Protein 11g; Fat 54g

INGREDIENTS:

5 OZ CUBED SALMON FILLET

2 CUPS ALMOND FLOUR

1 CUP CUBED COLD BUTTER

4 TBSP WHIPPING CREAM

2 LARGE EGGS AND 1 YOLK

1 LARGE AND FINELY SLICED GREEN ONION

1 TBSP LEMON JUICE

A PINCH OF BLACK PEPPER

DIRECTIONS:

1. Preheat the Air Fryer to 360° F., if needed.
2. Season salmon fillets with salt, pepper and lemon juice. Set it aside.
3. In a large bowl, stir in the butter.
4. Add the egg yolk, 1 tbsp. of water and knead the entire mixture into one ball. Roll the dough onto a floured hard surface.
5. Put the round dough into the quiche pan and seal on the edges.
6. Trim the dough to fit the edges of the pan you intend to use or just let it stick out. Beat eggs with cream, then add a pinch of salt and pepper.
7. Pour the mixture into the quiche pan, and add the green onions.
8. Slide the quiche pan in the Air Fryer's basket and set the timer to 20 minutes and the heat to 350° F.

Crested Halibut

Servings: 4

Prep + Cook Time: 30 minutes

NUTRITIONAL INFO PER SERVING:

Calories 287; Carbs 8.3g; Net Carbs 1.3g; Fiber 6.2g; Protein 22g; Fat 18g

INGREDIENTS:

¾ CUP PORK RINDS

4 HALIBUT FILLETS

½ CUP CHOPPED FRESH PARSLEY

¼ CUP CHOPPED FRESH DILL

¼ CUP CHOPPED FRESH CHIVES

1 TBSP EXTRA VIRGIN OLIVE OIL

1 TBSP FINELY GRATED LEMON ZEST

SEA SALT AND BLACK PEPPER

DIRECTIONS:

1. Preheat the Air Fryer to 390° F.
2. In a large bowl, mix the pork rinds, the parsley, the dill, the chives, the olive oil, the lemon zest, the sea salt, and black pepper.
3. Rinse the halibut fillets and dry them on a paper towel.
4. Arrange the halibut fillets on a baking sheet.
5. Spoon the rinds on the fish.
6. Lightly press the crumb mixture on the fillet.
7. Cook the fillets in a preheated Air Fryer's basket for 30 minutes.

Air Fried Catfish

Servings: 2

Prep + Cook Time: 20 minutes

NUTRITIONAL INFO PER SERVING:

Calories 365; Carbs 9.7g; Net Carbs 5.2g; Fiber 2.2g; Protein 33g; Fat 21g

INGREDIENTS:

2 CATFISH FILETS

A PINCH OF SALT

1 CUP BUTTERMILK

2 TBSP HOT SAUCE

2 TBSP OIL FOR SPRAYING

1 CUP ALMOND FLOUR

1 TBSP CRAB SEASONING

1 TBSP GARLIC POWDER

DIRECTIONS:

1. Season both sides of the catfish fillets with salt and pepper.
2. In a dish, combine the buttermilk with the hot sauce.
3. Add the catfish fillets and cover them with sufficient liquid. Let the ingredients soak while you prepare the rest of the ingredients.
4. Whisk all the ingredients, the flour, the crab seasoning and the garlic powder in a different casserole.
5. Remove the catfish from the buttermilk and let the excess oil drip off.
6. Now dredge the catfish on both sides with the almond flour mixture.
7. Place 2 of the fillets in the Air Fryer basket and drizzle with oil.
8. Set the temperature to 390° F and the time to 15 minutes.
9. When the cooking time is complete, open the basket, and gently turn the fillets, then spray oil and close the basket. Cook for 5 more minutes.

Air Fried Octopus with Chili

Servings: 3

Prep + Cook Time: 35 minutes

NUTRITIONAL INFO PER SERVING:

Calories 195; Carbs 7.3g; Net Carbs 4.2g; Fiber 0.2g; Protein 25g; Fat 7g

INGREDIENTS:

3 ROOTS WASHED CORIANDER

7 MEDIUM GREEN CHILIES

2 CLOVES GARLIC

A PINCH OF SALT

2 DROPS LIQUID STEVIA

2 SMALL LIMES

1 TBSP OLIVE OIL

1 LB CLEAN OCTOPUS

1 TSP FISH SAUCE

DIRECTIONS:

1. Mash the washed roots of coriander in the mortar.
2. Add the green chilies, the 2 cloves of garlic, a pinch of salt, stevia, 1 teaspoon of fish sauce, the juice of 2 limes and a teaspoon of olive oil.
3. Put the dipping sauce in a deep bowl.
4. Cut the octopus into tentacles.
5. Arrange the tentacles of the octopus in the Air Fryer basket and set the heat to 370° F.
6. Cook them for 4 minutes on each side.
7. Serve with the dipping sauce.

Yummy Halibut

Servings: 6

Prep + Cook Time: 35 minutes

NUTRITIONAL INFO PER SERVING:

Calories 432; Carbs 14.3g; Net Carbs 7.1g; Fiber 3.2g; Protein 27g; Fat 32g

INGREDIENTS:

2 LB HALIBUT FILLETS, CUT IN 6 PIECES

SALT AND BLACK PEPPER

3-4 CHOPPED GREEN ONIONS

½ CUP KETO MAYO

½ CUP SOUR CREAM

1 TBSP DRIED DILL WEED

DIRECTIONS:

1. Preheat the Air Fryer to 390° F, if needed.
2. Season the halibut with salt and pepper.
3. In a bowl, mix onions, mayonnaise, sour cream, and dill.
4. Spread the onion mixture evenly over the fish. Set the timer to 20 minutes and cook the Halibut.

Bacon Wrapped Shrimp

Servings: 16

Prep + Cook Time: 15 minutes

NUTRITIONAL INFO PER SERVING:

Calories 95; Carbs 5.3g; Net Carbs 3.2g; Fiber 0.5g; Protein 6g; Fat 7g

INGREDIENTS:

16 BUTTERFLIED KING SHRIMP

16 CHUNKS MONTERREY JACK CHEESE

16 COOKED BACON STRIPS

16 TOOTHPICKS

BARBECUE SAUCE, TO SERVE

DIRECTIONS:

5. Stuff one shrimp with one piece of cheese.

6. Close it and wrap it with a bacon strip, then secure it with a toothpick.

7. Repeat the same steps with the rest of the shrimps.

8. Cook them at 390° F for 5 minutes.

9. Shake the basket from time to time.

10. Serve the wrapped shrimp with the barbecue sauce.

Air Fried Spinach Fish

Servings: 2

Prep + Cook Time: 10 minutes

NUTRITIONAL INFO PER SERVING:

Calories 173; Carbs 2.3g; Net Carbs 0.5g; Fiber 1.2g; Protein 4g; Fat 18g

INGREDIENTS:

4 OZ SPINACH LEAVES

2 CUPS ALMOND FLOUR

A PINCH OF SALT

2 TBSP OIL

1 LARGE BEATEN EGG

DIRECTIONS:

1. In a deep bowl, add beaten egg, wheat flour, salt, and spinach leaves.

2. Marinate the fish. Cook in the Air Fryer for 12 minutes at 370° F.

3. Serve with lemon slices.

Roly Poly Air fried fish

Servings: 4

Prep + Cook Time: 12 minutes

NUTRITIONAL INFO PER SERVING:

Calories 267; Carbs 8.1g; Net Carbs 3.5g; Fiber 4.2g; Protein 39g; Fat 8g

INGREDIENTS:

2 LB WHITE FISH FILLETS

½ TBSP SALT

4 MUSHROOMS

1 TBSP LIQUID STEVIA

2 ONIONS

4 TBSP SOYA SAUCE

2 TBSP RED CHILI POWDER

2 TBSP VINEGAR

2 TBSP CHINESE WINTER PICKLE

DIRECTIONS:

1. Fill the fish with the pickle and the mushrooms.
2. Cut the onions into skinny slices then spread it on the fish.
3. Combine the vinegar, the stock, the soya sauce, the stevia, and the salt.
4. Sprinkle over the fish, and cook in the fryer for 10 minutes at 350° F.

Air Fried Dragon Shrimp

Servings: 2

Prep + Cook Time: 10 minutes

NUTRITIONAL INFO PER SERVING:

Calories 405; Carbs 9.3g; Net Carbs 5.2g; Fiber 3.2g; Protein 31g; Fat 27g

INGREDIENTS:

½ LB SHRIMP

½ CUP SOYA SAUCE

2 EGGS

2 TBSP OLIVE OIL

1 CUP CHOPPED ONIONS

A PINCH OF GINGER

¼ CUP ALMOND FLOUR

DIRECTIONS:

1. Boil the shrimps for around 5 minutes.
2. Meanwhile, prepare a paste made of ginger and onion.
3. Beat the eggs and add ginger, onion, soya sauce, corn flour and mix them very well.
4. Add shrimps to the mixture and cook them for 10 minutes, at 390° F.
5. Remove from the Air Fryer and serve with keto mayo.

Sweets and Desserts

Breton Butter Cake

Servings: 8

Prep + Cook Time: 20 minutes |

NUTRITIONAL INFO PER SERVING:

Calories 287; Carbs 1.3g; Net Carbs 0.8g; Fiber 0.2g; Protein 4g; Fat 31g

INGREDIENTS:

1 CUP BUTTER

¼ CUP LIQUID STEVIA

1 TBSP PURE VANILLA EXTRACT

6 EGG YOLKS

3 CUPS ALMOND FLOUR

¼ TSP SALT

1 LARGE AND LIGHTLY BEATEN EGG

DIRECTIONS:

1. Preheat the Air Fryer to 350° F, if needed.
2. In the bowl of an electric mixer, combine cream butter and stevia.
3. Keep mixing until it becomes fluffy.
4. Add vanilla and yolk gradually, and beat well after each yolk.
5. Now, transfer the batter into a 9-inch pan, with removable bottom.
6. Smooth the surface with a spatula.
7. Chill the batter in the fridge before baking it for 15 minutes.
8. Then brush it with a beaten egg and cook in the fryer for 35 minutes.

Lemon Cake

Servings: 16

Prep + Cook Time: 6 minutes

NUTRITIONAL INFO PER SERVING:

Calories 231; Carbs 0.3g; Net Carbs 0.1g; Fiber 0.1g; Protein 1.5g; Fat 27g

INGREDIENTS:

2 CUPS WARM BUTTER

¼ CUP LIQUID STEVIA

A PINCH OF SEA SALT

4 LARGE EGGS

1 GRATED AND UNTREATED LEMON RIND

2 CUPS ALMOND FLOUR

2 TBSP BAKING POWDER

DIRECTIONS:

1. Garnish the baking pan with a parchment paper or coat it with butter. Beat the warm butter, the stevia, and the salt.

2. Add eggs and lemon zest, and keep beating until the mixture becomes creamy and consistent. Sift in the flour and the baking powder.

3. Pour the batter into the baking pan. Cook at 320°F for 35 minutes.

Sponge Cake

Servings: 12

Prep + Cook Time: 40 minutes

NUTRITIONAL INFO PER SERVING:

Calories 183; Carbs 0.8g; Net Carbs 0.5g; Fiber 0.2g; Protein 1.7g; Fat 21g

INGREDIENTES:

1 CUP BUTTER

½ CUP LIQUID STEVIA

4 LARGE EGGS

2 CUPS ALMOND FLOUR

DIRECTIONS:

1. Preheat the Air Fryer to 350° F. Grease and flour a jelly roll pan.

2. In a deep bowl, cream butter and stevia until the mixture becomes light and soft. Beat in eggs, adding them one by one. Sift in flour and keep mixing until the batter becomes smooth. Spread the dough in the baking pan. Cook in the Air Fryer 350°F for 40 minutes.

Coconut Flour Bread

Servings: 6

Prep + Cook Time: 35 minutes

NUTRITIONAL INFO PER SERVING:

Calories 215; Carbs 1.3g; Net Carbs 0.6g; Fiber 0.3g; Protein 6.5g; Fat 22g

INGREDIENTS:

6 MEDIUM EGGS

½ TBSP ERYTHRITOL

½ CUP COCONUT OIL

¾ CUP COCONUT FLOUR

1 TBSP BAKING POWDER

DIRECTIONS:

1. Preheat the Air Fryer to 360° F, if needed. In a deep bowl, sift coconut flour, and add baking powder. Set aside.

2. In a separate bowl, mix the eggs, the oil, the erythritol and a pinch of salt. Add the dry ingredients and keep mixing until there are no lumps.

3. Spoon the batter into a greased loaf baking pan. Cook the dough in the Air Fryer for about 35 minutes.

Rolled Cookies

Servings: 8

Prep + Cook Time: 10 Minutes

NUTRITIONAL INFO PER SERVING:

Calories 341; Carbs 0.7g; Net Carbs 0.5g; Fiber 0.1g; Protein 3g; Fat 35g

INGREDIENTS:

1 ½ CUPS SOFTENED BUTTER

4 TBSP LIQUID STEVIA

4 LARGE EGGS

1 TBSP VANILLA EXTRACT

4 CUPS ALMOND FLOUR

2 TBSP BAKING POWDER

DIRECTIONS:

1. In a deep bowl, cream the butter and the stevia until smooth. Beat in the eggs and the vanilla. Add in flour, baking powder and 1 tsp of salt.

2. Cover the mixture and let chill for 2 hours. Preheat the Air Fryer to 390° F. Roll out the dough on a floured surface.

3. Cut the dough into cookies shapes. Arrange the cookies in the Air Fryer basket then cook them for around 10 minutes.

Pikelets

Servings: 8

Prep + Cook Time: 15 Minutes |

NUTRITIONAL INFO PER SERVING:

Calories 75; Carbs 1.3g; Net Carbs 0.6g; Fiber 0.5g; Protein 1.3g; Fat 7g

INGREDIENTS:

1 CUP ALMOND FLOUR

1 TBSP BAKING POWDER

1 LARGE EGG

1 TBSP LIQUID STEVIA

¾ CUP COCONUT MILK

DIRECTIONS

1. In a large bowl, sift in the flour and the baking powder.
2. In a separate bowl, beat eggs and stevia until they become thick.
3. Add the egg and pour in the milk until it is all combined.
4. Take a baking pan and line ramekins inside it.
5. Pour the batter evenly into the ramekins, making sure the poured mixture is thin. Cook the ramekins for 3 minutes at 325° F.
6. Serve the pikelets with butter or low-carb jam.

Made in the USA
San Bernardino, CA
24 December 2018